This Garden Journal
Belongs To:

My Growing Zone:

_____

Average Last Frost Date in Spring: _____

Average First Frost Date in Autumn: _____

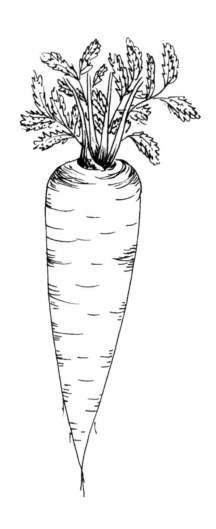

Contents

"If you have a garden and a library,
you have everything you need."

~ *Cicero*

Tips for Using this Journal

- Start with a quick bit of research to find your growing zone and the first and last frost dates for your location. Write this information on the blanks on the very first page of this journal so it will be very easy to find and refer back to.

- A garden does not need to be large or complicated. It can be as simple as a pot of mint on a windowsill (You can make tea with the leaves!), a jar of alfalfa sprouts, a tray of microgreens (Yummy in salads and sandwiches!), a small garden bed or a set of pots outdoors. Start wherever you are and with whatever you have!

- Check out a few books on gardening from your local library. You will find them very helpful if you are just getting started with growing plants for the first time. Among other things, books will help you to learn valuable information such as the differences between "good" and "bad" bugs for your garden, plants that are helpful to grow near each other (called "companion planting") and different methods for growing your plants (there are many).

- If at all possible, make a compost pile or bin (See page 8 for more information.). It is not difficult, and will be very helpful for building healthy soil. And it is quite fun!

- Pages 12 – 14 are for your garden "Wish List". This can be plants that you would like to try to grow in the future, or maybe a certain tool you would like to add to your gardening equipment.

- Pages 15-54 (the "Plant Record" pages) are for recording the details of each plant that you grow. Fill in the blank spaces with the necessary information and add a photo, if you would like to. Where the page lists "Date Planted", circle either "Seeds" or "Transplants" to note whether the plant was started from seed, or from a young plant ready to transplant into your garden space.

- On pages 55 – 87 you will find places to jot down various seasonal notes and things that need to be done in your garden. A few suggestions for these notes can be found on page 11.

- Beginning on page 89 are a few pages set aside for your garden layout ideas. It is helpful to sketch out your garden's layout (what is planted where) so that the following year you can change the placement of your crops. By rotating your plantings, you will keep both the soil and your plants healthier.

Soil & Seeds

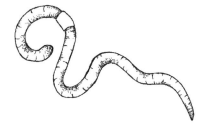

The soil is what anchors the roots of plants in place, as well as what supplies most of their water and nutrient needs. There are many different types of soils all over the earth. If we build healthy soil, the soil (with the help of a whole world of tiny animals and microorganisms) will feed the plants. Healthy soil is not compacted, but filled with millions of tiny pockets and tunnels (made by the beneficial creatures that live there) and will let air down into the soil and allow water flow through it at just the correct rate; not too fast and not too slow.

If we compress or pack down the garden soil by standing or sitting on it, we cause these little pockets and tunnels to collapse. It is especially important to never dig into the soil when it is very wet. This will compress and compact it quickly. Compressing the soil damages the soil life and makes it much harder for plants to grow. Good soil is teaming with life! Some of it is visible, and some we cannot see without a microscope.

An important part of good soil building is protecting any bare areas (that are not covered by plants) with mulch. Using mulch to cover the soil between and around plants keeps water from evaporating too quickly and helps the soil to stay moist and loose. Things such as straw, hay and fallen leaves all make very good mulches.

If you are growing your plants from seeds, pay close attention to the instructions on the back of the seed packet (This information will help your seeds get the strongest start possible.) and for best results, use a soil mixture made for starting seeds. Seeds can be started in any small recycled containers, small paper cups or even small pots made from newspaper (look up some of the many instructions online). The most important thing about these containers is that they have some way for the water to drain out of them. If your seedlings sit in water for a long period of time, they will rot. Many seedlings look alike when they are small so it is a good idea (whether you are starting your seeds in pots or in a garden bed), to make sure to label your seedlings so that you will know what you have planted where. Popsicle sticks and a permanent marker make very quick and easy garden markers, but just get creative and use whatever you have on hand!

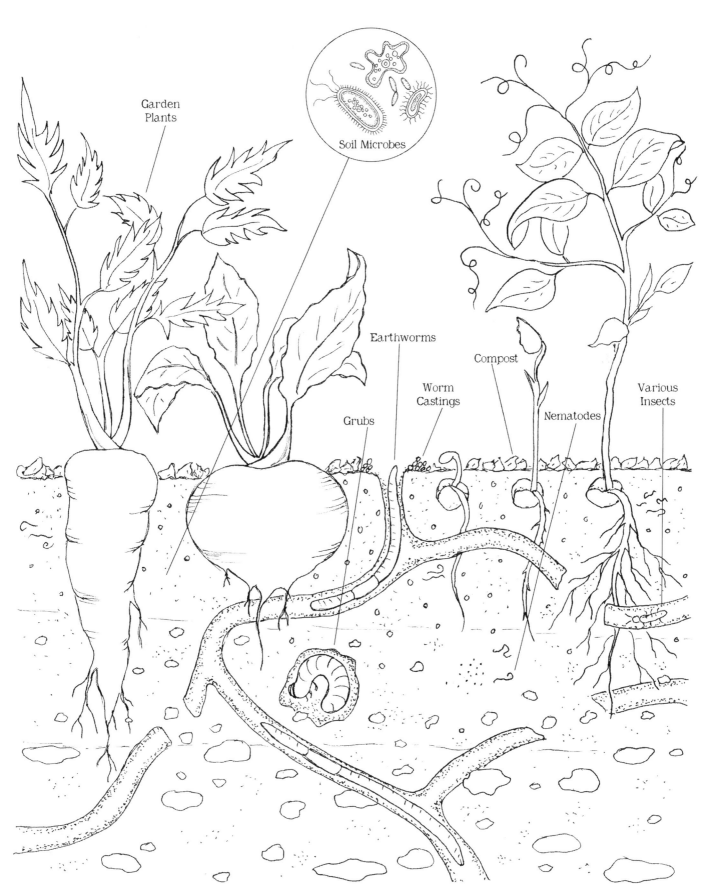

Garden
Plants

Soil Microbes

Earthworms

Worm
Castings

Compost

Grubs

Nematodes

Various
Insects

Compost

Compost is defined as "decayed organic matter used as a plant fertilizer". The term "organic matter" refers to anything that was once living. Composting is a wonderful way to recycle some of your food and yard (or garden) waste, while at the same time creating nutrient-rich soil that your plants will love. You do not need a giant pile to create nice compost. You can make small bin from an 18-gallon plastic tote (Which also works great as a worm bin if you should decide to try out "vermicomposting".) or a 32-gallon trash can. Compost only requires **carbon** ("brown" material), **nitrogen** ("green" material), **moisture**, **air** and **time**. To create a nice (and non-smelly) compost, there are just a few simple guidelines that should be followed:

1. When creating your compost bin, it is a good idea to drill a few small holes in the bottom of your tote or trash can so that excess liquid can drain out. Drilling several holes around the sides of the container will allow more airflow and you will not have to stir or turn your compost to aerate it as much. The holes are not absolutely necessary but will help speed up the decomposition process.

2. When collecting ingredients for your compost, try to shoot for a 30:1 ratio of browns (carbon) to greens (nitrogen), but compost-making is very flexible so consider this only a general guide. The 30:1 ratio simply means that for every thirty handfuls of browns (dried leaves, shredded paper, etc.), you should have one handful of greens (fresh grass clippings, vegetable scraps, etc.). Check out the list on the following page for ideas for your browns and greens. Shredding or chopping your materials will help them to break down faster.

3. Beginning and ending with browns, layer your materials in the bin. Every few layers, sprinkle the ingredients with water until everything is damp, but not soaking (like a wet, but not dripping, sponge). Adding a handful or two of soil is a great way to introduce those wonderful soil microorganisms that your mixture needs to be able to turn into compost. Replace the lid to your bin and simply give the bin a toss or stir about once a week to help aerate the mixture. Add a bit more water if it seems to be drying out over time.

4. As the microbes and other tiny creatures work to break down the materials into compost (over the course of 2 – 4 months, depending on the time of year and your ingredients), it will heat up and then cool down eventually shrinking to half its original volume as it begins to look more like soil and less like the original materials that went into it. To use your finished compost, simply sprinkle a handful around the base of your plants or work a bit into the soil of a new planting container. Compost is very nutrient-rich and a little goes a long way, so do not use more than 25% compost in your containers.

Browns
(Carbon)

Dried Leaves
Cardboard Egg Cartons
Shredded Paper
Straw & Hay
Pine Needles
Wood Ash
Saw Dust
Wood Chips or Shavings
Small Twigs
Tea Bags
Egg Shells
Old Fabric, Yarn or String (Natural
    Fibers Only)

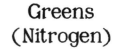

Greens
(Nitrogen)

Vegetable Scraps & Peelings
Fruit Scraps & Peelings
Used Coffee Grounds
Leaves from Weeds (Unsprayed!)
Fresh Grass Clippings
Wilted Flowers
Plant Trimmings from Garden
Manure from Herbivores

*Never Include Meat or
Dairy in Your Compost!*

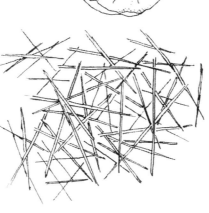

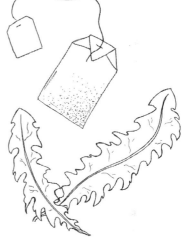

Compost Container Ideas

Useful Weeds

You do not want weeds growing in your garden and competing with your plants for the nutrients and water that they need, but the weeds that can be found in other areas of your yard can be quite useful. Many weeds have leaves and stems that are very high in nutrients and minerals (and some are even edible and medicinal!). For example, the leaves clover, chickweed, dandelion, dock, plantain, lamb's quarters, chicory, and more will be a valuable addition to your compost.

Never add the roots or seeds of weeds to your compost or garden! Some weeds reproduce from pieces of their roots, as well as from their seeds, and as useful as they may be, you do not want to fill your lovely garden with weeds.

Dandelion
Taraxacum officinale

A very useful weed! These pretty little plants are rich in potassium as well as other nutrients and minerals. The leaves of the dandelion make a great addition to your compost, but the plant is also useful in many other ways.

All parts of the dandelion plant are edible. The young leaves can be eaten fresh in salads, the blossoms can be made into jelly, tea or even fried as fritters. The roots of this plant can be used for a tea, or roasted and ground for a coffee substitute. The dandelion is also used medicinally!

Always make sure that the dandelions (or any other weeds) you pick have not been sprayed with any herbicides or pesticides!

Seasonal Suggestions

There are various things that need to be done at different times of the year for every garden. (Beginning on page 55 are a series of pages to make your own seasonal garden to-do lists.) Below you will find just a few ideas based on each season.

In the Spring:

Pull back mulch so that seeds can be sown and sprinkle a little compost on the top of the soil for the worms and other creatures to bring down to the lower layers of the soil. Plant seeds and seedlings at the correct time for your growing zone. Prepare new beds and pull out any weeds that emerge as the weather begins to warm.

In the Summer:

Sprinkle compost around plants and spread mulch around them to keep ground moist and soft. Pull out any weeds that have sprouted. A good layer of mulch will also discourage weeds. In late summer, start seeds for autumn grown plants.

In the Autumn:

Save seeds from flowers and plants that have gone to seed. Sow seeds, or plant out young plants, of any cool weather vegetables, herbs or flowers. Cover any bare soil (with nothing planted in it) with mulch for the winter. Plant any spring-flowering bulbs at this time.

In the Winter:

Cover any bare soil with mulch for the winter. Look through seed catalogs and plan what you would like to plant the following season. (When you are thinking about what you would like to plant, consider planting something for the pollinators!) In late winter, begin any seeds indoors that will not be directly sown in the garden. Pull mulch back and sprinkle compost over the soil, then recover it with mulch until you are ready to plant. Make garden markers with the plant names on them.

Garden Wish List

Garden Wish List

Garden Wish List

My Plant Records

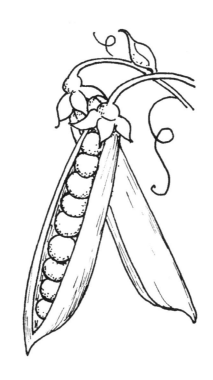

Plant Record

Common Name:

Botanical Name:

Description:

Date Planted (Seeds / Transplant):

Date Harvested:

Pests or Problems:

Special Care Needed:

Other Notes:

(Paste Photo Here)

Plant Record

Common Name:

Botanical Name:

Description:

Date Planted (Seeds / Transplant):

Date Harvested:

Pests or Problems:

Special Care Needed:

Other Notes:

(Paste Photo Here)

Plant Record

Common Name:

Botanical Name:

Description:

Date Planted (Seeds / Transplant):

Date Harvested:

Pests or Problems:

Special Care Needed:

Other Notes:

(Paste Photo Here)

Plant Record

Common Name:

Botanical Name:

Description:

Date Planted (Seeds / Transplant):

Date Harvested:

Pests or Problems:

Special Care Needed:

Other Notes:

(Paste Photo Here)

Plant Record

Common Name:

Botanical Name:

Description:

Date Planted (Seeds / Transplant):

Date Harvested:

Pests or Problems:

Special Care Needed:

(Paste Photo Here)

Other Notes:

 Plant Record

Common Name:

Botanical Name:

Description:

Date Planted (Seeds / Transplant):

Date Harvested:

Pests or Problems:

Special Care Needed:

Other Notes:

(Paste Photo Here)

Plant Record

Common Name:

Botanical Name:

Description:

Date Planted (Seeds / Transplant):

Date Harvested:

Pests or Problems:

Special Care Needed:

Other Notes:

(Paste Photo Here)

Plant Record

Common Name:

Botanical Name:

Description:

Date Planted (Seeds / Transplant):

Date Harvested:

Pests or Problems:

Special Care Needed:

Other Notes:

(Paste Photo Here)

 # Plant Record

Common Name:

Botanical Name:

Description:

Date Planted (Seeds / Transplant):

Date Harvested:

Pests or Problems:

Special Care Needed:

Other Notes:

(Paste Photo Here)

Plant Record

Common Name:

Botanical Name:

Description:

Date Planted (Seeds / Transplant):

Date Harvested:

Pests or Problems:

Special Care Needed:

Other Notes:

(Paste Photo Here)

Plant Record

Common Name:

Botanical Name:

Description:

Date Planted (Seeds / Transplant):

Date Harvested:

Pests or Problems:

Special Care Needed:

Other Notes:

(Paste Photo Here)

 Plant Record

Common Name:

Botanical Name:

Description:

Date Planted (Seeds / Transplant):

Date Harvested:

Pests or Problems:

Special Care Needed:

(Paste Photo Here)

Other Notes:

Plant Record

Common Name: _____

Botanical Name: _____

Description: _____

_____

Date Planted (Seeds / Transplant): _____

Date Harvested: _____

Pests or Problems: _____

_____

_____

Special Care Needed: _____

_____

_____

_____

_____

(Paste Photo Here)

Other Notes: _____

_____

_____

_____

_____

_____

_____

_____

_____

Plant Record

Common Name:

Botanical Name:

Description:

Date Planted (Seeds / Transplant):

Date Harvested:

Pests or Problems:

Special Care Needed:

Other Notes:

(Paste Photo Here)

Plant Record

Common Name:

Botanical Name:

Description:

Date Planted (Seeds / Transplant):

Date Harvested:

Pests or Problems:

Special Care Needed:

Other Notes:

(Paste Photo Here)

Plant Record

Common Name:

Botanical Name:

Description:

Date Planted (Seeds / Transplant):

Date Harvested:

Pests or Problems:

Special Care Needed:

(Paste Photo Here)

Other Notes:

Plant Record

Common Name:

Botanical Name:

Description:

Date Planted (Seeds / Transplant):

Date Harvested:

Pests or Problems:

Special Care Needed:

(Paste Photo Here)

Other Notes:

Plant Record

Common Name:

Botanical Name:

Description:

Date Planted (Seeds / Transplant):

Date Harvested:

Pests or Problems:

Special Care Needed:

Other Notes:

(Paste Photo Here)

Plant Record

Common Name:

Botanical Name:

Description:

Date Planted (Seeds / Transplant):

Date Harvested:

Pests or Problems:

Special Care Needed:

Other Notes:

(Paste Photo Here)

Plant Record

Common Name:

Botanical Name:

Description:

Date Planted (Seeds / Transplant):

Date Harvested:

Pests or Problems:

Special Care Needed:

Other Notes:

(Paste Photo Here)

 Plant Record

Common Name:

Botanical Name:

Description:

Date Planted (Seeds / Transplant):

Date Harvested:

Pests or Problems:

Special Care Needed:

Other Notes:

(Paste Photo Here)

Plant Record

Common Name:

Botanical Name:

Description:

Date Planted (Seeds / Transplant):

Date Harvested:

Pests or Problems:

Special Care Needed:

Other Notes:

(Paste Photo Here)

Plant Record

Common Name:

Botanical Name:

Description:

Date Planted (Seeds / Transplant):

Date Harvested:

Pests or Problems:

Special Care Needed:

Other Notes:

(Paste Photo Here)

 Plant Record

Common Name:

Botanical Name:

Description:

Date Planted (Seeds / Transplant):

Date Harvested:

Pests or Problems:

Special Care Needed:

Other Notes:

(Paste Photo Here)

 Plant Record

Common Name:

Botanical Name:

Description:

Date Planted (Seeds / Transplant):

Date Harvested:

Pests or Problems:

Special Care Needed:

Other Notes:

(Paste Photo Here)

 Plant Record

Common Name:

Botanical Name:

Description:

Date Planted (Seeds / Transplant):

Date Harvested:

Pests or Problems:

Special Care Needed:

Other Notes:

(Paste Photo Here)

Plant Record

Common Name:

Botanical Name:

Description:

Date Planted (Seeds / Transplant):

Date Harvested:

Pests or Problems:

Special Care Needed:

Other Notes:

(Paste Photo Here)

 Plant Record

Common Name:

Botanical Name:

Description:

Date Planted (Seeds / Transplant):

Date Harvested:

Pests or Problems:

Special Care Needed:

Other Notes:

(Paste Photo Here)

Plant Record

Common Name:

Botanical Name:

Description:

Date Planted (Seeds / Transplant):

Date Harvested:

Pests or Problems:

Special Care Needed:

Other Notes:

(Paste Photo Here)

Plant Record

Common Name:

Botanical Name:

Description:

Date Planted (Seeds / Transplant):

Date Harvested:

Pests or Problems:

Special Care Needed:

Other Notes:

(Paste Photo Here)

Plant Record

Common Name:

Botanical Name:

Description:

Date Planted (Seeds / Transplant):

Date Harvested:

Pests or Problems:

Special Care Needed:

Other Notes:

(Paste Photo Here)

# Plant Record

Common Name:

Botanical Name:

Description:

Date Planted (Seeds / Transplant):

Date Harvested:

Pests or Problems:

Special Care Needed:

Other Notes:

(Paste Photo Here)

Plant Record

Common Name:

Botanical Name:

Description:

Date Planted (Seeds / Transplant):

Date Harvested:

Pests or Problems:

Special Care Needed:

Other Notes:

(Paste Photo Here)

 *Plant Record*

Common Name:

Botanical Name:

Description:

Date Planted (Seeds / Transplant):

Date Harvested:

Pests or Problems:

Special Care Needed:

(Paste Photo Here)

Other Notes:

 Plant Record

Common Name:

Botanical Name:

Description:

Date Planted (Seeds / Transplant):

Date Harvested:

Pests or Problems:

Special Care Needed:

(Paste Photo Here)

Other Notes:

Plant Record

Common Name:

Botanical Name:

Description:

Date Planted (Seeds / Transplant):

Date Harvested:

Pests or Problems:

Special Care Needed:

(Paste Photo Here)

Other Notes:

Plant Record

Common Name:

Botanical Name:

Description:

Date Planted (Seeds / Transplant):

Date Harvested:

Pests or Problems:

Special Care Needed:

(Paste Photo Here)

Other Notes:

Plant Record

Common Name:

Botanical Name:

Description:

Date Planted (Seeds / Transplant):

Date Harvested:

Pests or Problems:

Special Care Needed:

(Paste Photo Here)

Other Notes:

Plant Record

Common Name:

Botanical Name:

Description:

Date Planted (Seeds / Transplant):

Date Harvested:

Pests or Problems:

Special Care Needed:

(Paste Photo Here)

Other Notes:

Seasonal Notes

Spring

Seasonal Garden Notes & To-Do's
Spring

Seasonal Garden Notes & To-Do's
Spring

Seasonal Garden Notes & To-Do's
Spring

Seasonal Garden Notes & To-Do's
Spring

Seasonal Garden Notes & To-Do's
Spring

Seasonal Garden Notes & To-Do's
Spring

Seasonal Garden Notes & To-Do's
Spring

Summer

Seasonal Garden Notes & To-Do's
Summer

Seasonal Garden Notes & To-Do's
Summer

Seasonal Garden Notes & To-Do's
Summer

Seasonal Garden Notes & To-Do's
Summer

Seasonal Garden Notes & To-Do's
Summer

Seasonal Garden Notes & To-Do's
Summer

Seasonal Garden Notes & To-Do's
Summer

Autumn

Seasonal Garden Notes & To-Do's
Autumn

Seasonal Garden Notes & To-Do's
Autumn

Seasonal Garden Notes & To-Do's
Autumn

Seasonal Garden Notes & To-Do's
Autumn

Seasonal Garden Notes & To-Do's
Autumn

Seasonal Garden Notes & To-Do's
Autumn

Seasonal Garden Notes & To-Do's
Autumn

Winter

Seasonal Garden Notes & To-Do's
Winter

Seasonal Garden Notes & To-Do's
Winter

Seasonal Garden Notes & To-Do's
Winter

Seasonal Garden Notes & To-Do's
Winter

Seasonal Garden Notes & To-Do's
Winter

Seasonal Garden Notes & To-Do's
Winter

Seasonal Garden Notes & To-Do's
Winter

"However many years she lived, Mary always felt that 'she should never forget that first morning when her garden began to grow'."

~ Frances Hodgson Burnett,
The Secret Garden

Garden Layout
Ideas

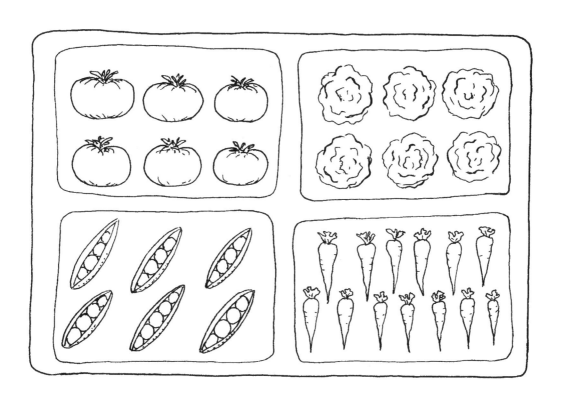

 # Garden Layout Ideas

 # Garden Layout Ideas

 # Garden Layout Ideas

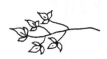 # Garden Layout Ideas

 # Garden Layout Ideas

 # Garden Layout Ideas

 # Garden Layout Ideas

 # Garden Layout Ideas

 # Garden Layout Ideas

 # Garden Layout Ideas

 # Garden Layout Ideas

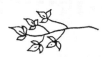 # Garden Layout Ideas

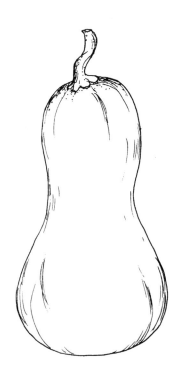